The Bubble Book

by Lisa Feder-Feitel
Illustrated by Patricia Hammel

W9-BMH-113

SCHOLASTIC INC.
New York   Toronto   London   Auckland   Sydney

For Cecily and Nick, my bubbly children,
and for Charlie, the source of my own effervescence.

Many thanks to The Exploratorium (San Francisco, CA), The Liberty Science
Center (Jersey City, NJ), The Nature Company, and The Children's
Museum (Boston, MA) for their research assistance.

ISBN 0-590-48280-7

12 11 10 9 8 7 6 5 4 3 2 1   4 5 6 7 8/9

Printed in the U.S.A.   24

First Scholastic printing, May 1994

Contents

Welcome to the World of Bubbles!

Shining, soaring, floating free,
Each holds a rainbow I can see!
I blow so gently — then I stop . . .
And watch until each one goes *POP*!

A Super Bubble Recipe

Making bubbles is easy. Here's what you need.

One clean bucket or pan

One mixing spoon

8 tablespoons of dishwashing liquid

One quart of cool, clean water

One tablespoon of glycerine (The glycerine makes the bubbles last longer. You can get this at a drugstore.)

Gently stir the soap, water, and glycerine in the pail.

Then let your bubble mix sit for a few minutes. The longer you let it sit, the better — and bubblier — it gets!

Dip your wand into the bubble mix. Make sure to dip it deeply, so that the star is all soapy. Wave your wand and watch the bubbles float away!

What Is a Bubble?

Catch a bubble on your wand.

What exactly is a bubble?

A bubble is a ball of air, with a thin, stretchy skin around it. Around a soap bubble, that skin is made of soap and water. The soap makes the bubble skin very stretchy.

When you blow into a wand wet with bubble mix, you push air against the bubble's skin.

Just like when you blow up a balloon, the rubbery skin stretches as it fills with air. When you blow a bubble, its soapy skin stretches, too — and makes a round bubble.

Why Is a Bubble Round?

The wand that came with this book is shaped like a star.

Dip it into the bubble mix, and wave the wand gently through the air.

What shape are the bubbles?

Bubbles are always round! Bubbles are round because of something called **surface tension.**

Surface tension is a force that pulls the soapy skin of the bubble into a sphere.

A sphere is the shape of a globe, or an orange, or a baseball . . . or every bubble you'll ever blow!

Try to catch a bubble on your soapy palm. See what happens?

The bubble stays half-round. It becomes a hemisphere!

Sometimes the wind will change the shape of a bubble. For a moment, it may look more like a sausage than a sphere. But the bubble will return to its round shape — if it doesn't pop first!

Why Do Bubbles Float?

In the air, bubbles float because they are very light. Remember, they are made mostly of air! Bubbles soar and drift, lifted by moving air.

But what goes up will come down, because of another force called **gravity.** Gravity pulls everything back to earth.

Try launching a bubble straight toward the sky. It will slowly come downward — if it doesn't pop first.

Why don't bubbles sink in the tub?

Water has a special force that keeps bubbles floating. That force is called **buoyancy** (BOY-an-see). It pushes the bubbles up, and keeps them on the water's surface.

You can see this force at work!

In your bathtub, push a rubber duck or ball down to the bottom of the tub. Now watch closely!

The water will push the toy back up to the water's surface. Water does the same thing to bubbles to make them float!

The Colors of a Bubble

Have you ever seen a rainbow?
Every bubble has a rainbow of colors on its surface.
Blow a bubble and take a very close look.
A kaleidoscope of colors swirls across it.
Light makes the colors of a bubble shine. Light reflects, or bounces, off both sides of a bubble's soapy skin, inside and out.

When the reflections meet, they create the colors we see.

The swirling shows us that the skin of the bubble is thicker and thinner in different places.

Catch a bubble. Watch the colors swirl.

After a while, the swirling colors disappear. The bubble looks black!

Can you guess what happens next?

The bubble pops because its skin is too thin!

Different Bubble Makers

You can find things around your house that make great bubbles — in your kitchen, your closet, maybe even in your garbage!

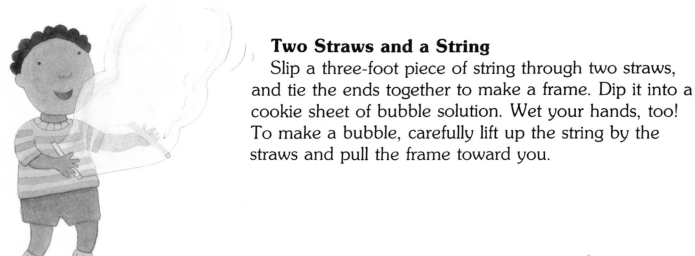

Two Straws and a String

Slip a three-foot piece of string through two straws, and tie the ends together to make a frame. Dip it into a cookie sheet of bubble solution. Wet your hands, too! To make a bubble, carefully lift up the string by the straws and pull the frame toward you.

The Bubble "Tube-a"

Find an empty cardboard tube, like the ones used for paper towels. Gently dip one end of the tube into bubble mix. When you see a film of soap there, you're ready to blow. Hold the tube about two inches from your mouth and slowly blow through it.

A Six-pack of Bubbles

The linked plastic loops that hold soda and juice cans together make it easy to carry those cans. They make great bubbles, too! Just dip the loops into bubble mix and wave it around. *Whee!* Bubbles galore!

A Coat Hanger Loop

With a grown-up's help, bend a coat hanger into a circle. Fill a large pan with bubble mix and dip the loop in.

Wave your large loop gently through the air and launch your own big bubbles!

Bubble Experiments

Here are some bubble feats to amaze your entire family!

A Chain of Bubbles

Pour some bubble mix into a shallow pan or cookie sheet. Dip one end of a plain drinking straw into the pan, and remove it. Now hold the straw just above the pan, and gently blow as you move the straw along the surface. You will see a small chain of bubbles! Try again.

A Bubble Inside a Bubble

There is another experiment with a straw and bubble mix in a pan. Dip one end of the straw in the mix, and blow a good-sized bubble on the surface. Slip the straw downward into the bubble and blow again. It's a bubble inside a bubble!

The Shape of Things to Come

Get some pipe cleaners. Bend them into different shapes, such as spirals, knots, and curves. As you dip a shape into the solution, take a guess. What will the soap film on each shape look like when you pull it out? What will happen when you blow a bubble? What shape do you think it will be?

See the Pyramids! (This one's hard!)

Free-floating bubbles are always round, but you can make other shapes — such as a pyramid. You need six pipe cleaners and bubble mix. Bend and twist the pipe cleaners into a pyramid shape. Soak the frame in bubble solution. As long as the frame is wet, the bubble will hold the frame's shape.

Bubbles Are Everywhere!

Bubbles are all around us — and everyone from firefighters to fish find them handy!

Fish need bubbles to breathe. The air bubbling into an aquarium enters the water as tiny bubbles and helps the fish breathe.

People blow bubbles when they swim. Remember when you learned to swim? Blowing bubbles in the water was one of your first lessons. Swimmers turn their heads to breathe air in, then blow bubbles into the water to let the air out.

Soap bubbles help dishwashers scrub dirt away. As you wash dishes, the soap mixes with the grease and makes it easier to wipe the grease off the dish. Then the grease floats away in the water!

Firefighters use foam made of tiny bubbles to put out certain fires. The foam keeps air from reaching the fire.

Bubbles make your soda *pop*! When you sip soda, the fizz that tickles your tongue is made of little bubbles. A gas called **carbon dioxide** (CAR-bun di-OX-side) gives soda its fizz!

When this gas is trapped with water in a closed soda can, it mixes with the water — but the pressure builds.

Open the top of a soda can, and what do you see?

The gas escapes — and out come those tiny bubbles!

Scientists Study Bubbles

Scientists who study bubbles are called **bubbleologists.** Bubbles can teach scientists many things about the environment.

Bubbleologists look at the bubbles in ocean waves and raindrops. These bubbles teach scientists about the earth's weather.

Tiny bubbles trapped in ancient fossils help scientists learn about why dinosaurs became extinct. Bubbleologists also study bubbles in Antarctic ice, and even in outer space!

One famous bubbleologist is Eiffel Plasterer. For more than fifty years, he performed amazing bubble experiments at science fairs and museums around the country.

He made four-foot-long bubble chains and brightly colored bubble castles. He blew bubbles inside of bubbles inside of bubbles. He even put people inside of bubbles!

Science Museums: Explore Bubbles

At science and children's museums, you can experiment with bubbles as bubbleologists do.

Here are some ways to discover the wonders of bubbles. Most of them you can do at home!

Make a Bubble Wall

Fill a shallow pan with bubble mix. Attach two pieces of string to a pair of wooden sticks. Now soak the string and both sticks in bubble mix. Wet your hands, too! After a minute, slowly lift the top stick — and the string — from the mix. *Ta-DA!*

You have created a sheer wall of bubble. Look through its soapy window.

What do you see? Wave the top bar or gently blow on your bubble — and watch to see how long it takes before it pops!

Catch the Wave

Make a square, a triangle, or any shape you like by bending pipe cleaners. Use an extra pipe cleaner to make a handle on each shape.

Dip your shape into bubble mix, and hang it near a light. As the light shines through the soap film, watch the colors shimmer. Then tap the hanging shape and see the bubble really wave and wiggle!

Measure for Measure

Fill a shallow pan with bubble mix. Use a cardboard tube or straw to blow a half-bubble — or hemisphere — on the pan's surface.

Once you've blown it, you can measure it! Wet a plastic ruler with bubble solution, and gently slip it into the center of the bubble. Now read it. How big is your bubble?

Fun Facts about Bubbles

You've learned a lot of facts about bubbles from reading this book, but here are even more to make you wonder.

How Big Was It?

On June 6, 1988, in New York City, David Stein blew a bubble that was fifty feet long! He made this enormous bubble using a bubble wand (just like yours), dishwashing liquid, and water.

An Oldie but Goodie

Using a special bubble solution that he invented, bubbleologist Eiffel Plasterer once made a bubble that lasted 304 days. Stored in a tightly sealed jar in his basement, the bubble shrank as it aged. Finally, it grew very tiny — and popped!

Every Shape Under the Sun

Tom Noddy is a bubble artist. He creates bubbles inside of bubbles, inside-out bubbles, bubble cubes, and bubble caterpillars. He even makes carousel bubbles — bubbles that spin inside of other bubbles! Most amazing of all, he does all his artwork with just bubble mix and a little plastic wand!

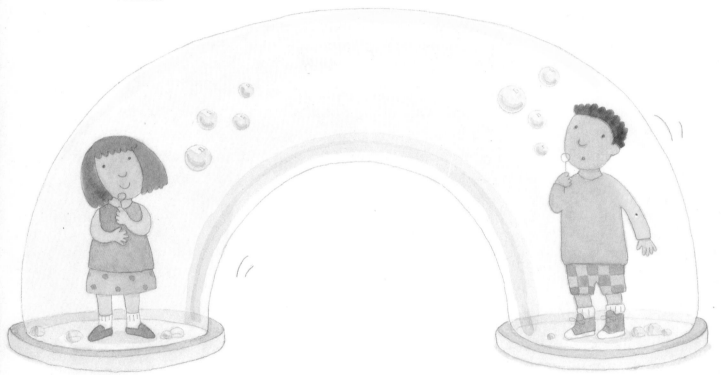

Under the Rainbow

Bubbleologist Richard Faverty once blew a bubble arch. It was so big that two bubble-blowing children could stand inside. It lasted seven seconds — and popped when it touched the kids' heads!

Bubbles Are Fun for Everyone!

You don't have to be a bubbleologist to have fun with bubbles.

What's the best thing about bubbles? Everything!

You can take them anywhere. A jar of bubble soap with a wand will fit in your pocket or backpack.

You can play with bubbles outside or in — especially in the tub.

Bubbles are easy to make. All you need is soap and water. Then you just wet your wand and wave it around.

Bubbles make you smile. Whether you're alone or with friends, bubbles have this funny way of making you grin. Try blowing some and see. If you don't smile, a bubble may land on your nose and tickle you before it pops!

Bubble Games

In the park, your yard, or even in the bathtub, there are many ways to have fun with bubbles. Here are a few games to get you started. Once you get blowing, the sky's the limit!

Bubble Catch

Launch a bubble and try to catch it again with your wand. How many times can you catch, blow, and catch again?

Does the bubble change in any way? Try to launch a bubble to a wand-holding friend. Can he or she catch it and blow it back to you?

Bubble Race

Mark a starting and a finish line and find a bubble-blowing friend. Now, launch your bubbles. Whose bubble crosses the finish line first?

Time the Bubbles

Use a stopwatch to time your bubble creations. How long did your longest bubble last? Your shortest? Try the same game at different times of day. Try to set a new record each time!

Count the Bubbles

Next time you're in a bubbly tub, try counting the bubbles around you. How many can you blow with one steady breath?

Bubble-Blowing Tips

Wind, water, and even a speck of dust can mean big trouble for bubbles. Here are some tips to help keep you blowing your best.

Wet is best. Keep everything that touches your bubbles wet: your wand, your hands, a ruler, and so on. Even a dry finger will burst a bubble.

Cool and shady areas are good for making bubbles. Foggy or cloudy days — or after a rain — are great bubble days. On dry days, try blowing near trees, grass, or bushes. Green leaves send wetness into the air.

Watch out for the wind. A strong breeze will burst bubbles almost before you blow them. Try to stand with the wind at your back or find a calm place where the air is still.

Save leftover suds. Pour your bubble solution into a jar and close it tightly. Store it in a dark, cool place. The longer the bubble mix sits, the better it gets!